SHARKS

GALLERY BOOKS
An Imprint of W. H. Smith Publishers Inc.
112 Madison Avenue
New York City 10016

This edition first published in U.S.
in 1990 by Gallery Books,
an imprint of W. H. Smith Publishers, Inc.
112 Madison Avenue, New York, New York 10016

ISBN 0-8317-9579-4

Printed and bound in Spain

For rights information about the photographs in
this book please contact:

The Image Bank
111 Fifth Avenue, New York, NY 10003

Producer: Solomon M. Skolnick
Author: Lee Server
Design Concept: Lesley Ehlers
Designer: Ann-Louise Lipman
Editor: Terri L. Hardin
Production: Valerie Zars
Photo Researcher: Edward Douglas
Editorial Assistant: Carol Raguso
Assistant Photo Researcher: Robert Hale

Title page: **In legend, the shark is a ruthless killing machine, the personification of evil. In reality, sharks are creatures of great diversity and intelligence, and only rarely harmful to humans.** *Opposite:* **Despite its awkward appearance, the hammerhead (genus *Sphyrna*) is one of the fastest and most agile of sharks. Its lateral-shaped head serves as a forward planing surface in the water.**

Preceding page: There are in nine species of hammerhead shark, including the scalloped hammerhead *(Sphyrna lewini)*. With its eyes placed on either end of its stalk-like head, the hammerhead must continually twist from side to side in order to see ahead. *This page:* The hammerhead can grow to as large as 15 feet, and is common to temperate and tropical coastal waters.

Sharks have existed for an estimated 450 million years. They swam the earth's seas before and all through the rise and fall of the dinosaurs, and hundreds of millions of years before man first trod on dry land. Despite the extinction of species and evolutionary developments since the earliest known fossil records, the design of the shark is relatively unchanged. Of all the creatures from prehistory, the shark is surely among the few still thriving in the late twentieth century.

In this rare photograph taken in New England waters, a baby requiem shark is seen. ("Requiem" is a term used for sharks of the Carcharhinid family.) *Below:* Born prematurely and with its egg sac still attached, this shark is already swimming on its own, in search of food.

The sand tiger shark (Family Odontaspididae) can grow to over 10 feet in length. Unlike its cousin, the tiger shark *(Galeocerdo cuvier)*, the sand tiger is not very dangerous to humans. *Overleaf:* The diversity of the shark includes a wide variety of tooth designs. The type of tooth for a particular shark species is connected to its normal prey. Here, a sand tiger shark reveals his sharp, pointy incisors.

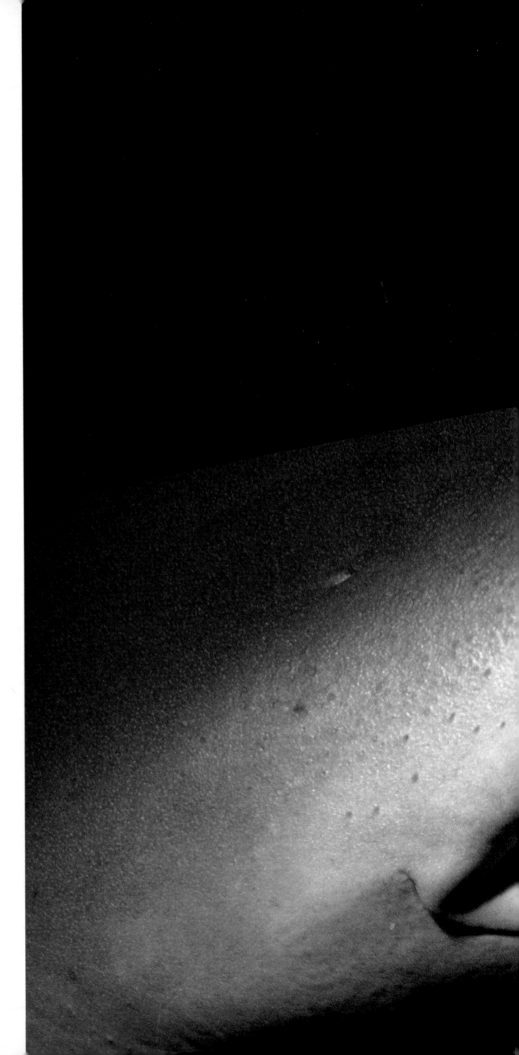

The development of the modern predatory sharks seems tied in with the appearance of large, aquatic mammals – porpoises, seals, sea lions, whales – after the last of the dinosaurs. It is in this period – approximately 60 million years ago – that we find the remains of some of the first makos and great whites, the man-eaters of today.

Until recent times, it had been a long-held belief that all sharks had the same narrow set of characteristics. It was believed that because of their being relatively unchanged from the earliest times, sharks were primitive creatures; mindless and aggressive brutes.

In fact, sharks are quite varied in size and shape, with some species, like the angel shark or the hammerhead, evidencing extreme modifications of what we tend to think of as the "classic type" shark. Furthermore, sharks have brains and body systems of some sophistication: they are capable of much retention of knowledge, and their behavior is the result of complex interaction between hearing, sight, smell, and electrosenses.

It was, as well, falsely believed that all sharks were lone predators, cruising the seas in solitude except for short mating sessions. Actually, while some species like the great white spend most of all their lives alone, a number of other species (again, the hammerhead is an example) will travel in schools, or groups, of their own kind.

Like a number of other fishes, sharks practice social segregation by size (smaller sharks steering clear of larger ones), but they also have been known to practice sexual segregation. In some species, such as the blue shark, male sharks may spend the summer in warmer waters while females go to the chillier waters in the north. And what of the belief that the large, predatory species – the *requiem* or whaler sharks – were constant swimmers?

The photographs on this page show the tiger shark *(Galeocerdo cuvier)*, a fierce predator. It is one of the most dangerous sharks as it can grow to more than 17 feet in length, will devour anything (including humans), and frequently feeds in shallow water. Luckily, it does not often leave deep waters until nighttime.

A grey reef shark *(Carcharhinus amblyrhynchos)* cruises above a coral promontory. The reef, with its strong current and concentration of prey, makes a good hunting ground.

The grey reef shark *(Carcharhinus amblyrhynchos)* is prone to the notorious "feeding frenzy." At an average length of five feet, the grey reef is not one of the larger sharks, but its aggressive side can be so easily triggered that it is certainly one of the most violent and dangerous. A feeding frenzy can be set off by a single drop of blood in the water. *Below:* A solitary grey reef shark.

Easily identified, the whitetip reef shark *(Triaenodon obesus)* **has the tips of its upper tail-lobe and first dorsal fin splashed a bright white.**

Part of the shark's demonic image was this popular notion that it was cursed to swim the seas forever, its entire life, never stopping, never sleeping. We now know that these sharks may gather in dormitory-like caves where influxes of fresh water occur, and they will tranquilly rest or sleep, sometimes piled atop each other as if in bunk beds.

Obviously, the concept of the shark as no more than a brainless killer is woefully out of date. The shark is a most complicated creature and many of its capabilities are only just becoming understood by science.

There are approximately 350 different species of shark. Although sharks represent just one percent of all species of fish, that percentage may be increasing while you read this. Many new species have been found in recent years, including one exceptional find: the discovery of the megamouth shark. Indeed, less than 20 years ago, the total number of species was thought to be only 250.

Sharks differ from the majority of fish in that their skeleton is not made of bone but of cartilage. (Cartilaginous fish include only sharks, rays, skates, and chimaeras.) Cartilage is the rubbery, collagen-based material

The whitetip reef shark *(Triaenodon obesus)* is relatively harmless. Common to the Indian Ocean and Pacific waters, it spends most of the day lying in the open on the ocean floor.

The face of an angel—an angel shark, that is. With its flattish body and pectoral fins and its "wavy" swimming style, the angel (genus *Squatina*) seems more like a ray than a shark. *Opposite:* A diver observes an angel shark. The angel is a bottom-dweller, often burying itself in sand. It feeds on a diet of sea snails, squid, and bivalves, among other delicacies.

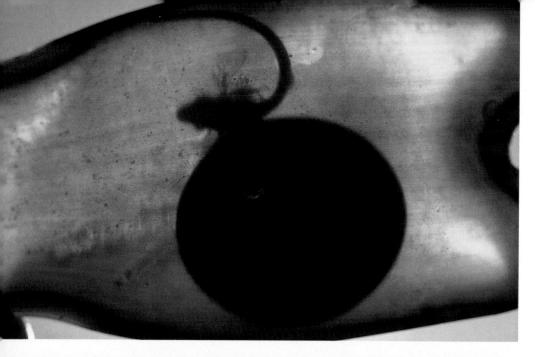

we find in our own bodies in the nose and ears. It is a more flexible material than bone – which it becomes with the addition of calcium phosphate deposits. In the water, the shark's cartilaginous skeleton makes for the graceful and sinuous swimming style with which we associate it, but out of the water it is severely strained. A shark can be crushed to death by its own weight.

Because cartilage precedes bone in skeletal development – cartilage turning into bone through ossification – it was at one time believed that fish may have been an evolutionary outgrowth of sharks. This enhanced the idea that the shark was a "primitive," unevolved fish, unchanged from the dawn of creation. Actually, the bony fish predated the arrival of the shark and developed quite independently. At any rate, the advantage of a cartilaginous skeleton is a lighter and more flexible frame, and is necessary to sharks' survival.

Because sharks do not have the gas-filled swim bladder of fish, they must have as minimally

Top to bottom: The swellshark (genus *Cephaloscyllium*) develops for 10 months inside a resilient, green-gold egg case, feeding on the attached egg yolk. Upon hatching, the baby swellshark begins swimming immediately in its first search for food – primarily tiny crustaceans at this stage. The swellshark will grow to about four feet in length. It will spend most of its life on the ocean floor, inhaling sleeping fish through its large, gaping mouth. *Opposite:* Eyesight is variable among sharks. Active swimming predators tend to have large eyes, while slower, bottom-dwelling sharks, such as this swellshark, have smaller eyes.

Preceding pages: The intimidating smile of a shark. The complex design of the shark includes an almost endless supply of teeth, which grow in a "tooth bed." When one tooth is broken off, a new one moves up into its place. *This page:* Getting a shark to pose for a closeup (top) is not easy; in fact, underwater conditions make it necessary for the photographer to work within six or seven feet of the subject—a potentially deadly perspective. Bottom-dwellers (bottom), less aggressive and often immobile, are more cooperative subjects for the photographer.

dense a body as possible in order to move freely in the water. Their oily livers keep their buoyancy neutral. In other words, while the shark will sink if it stops swimming, it can also propel its low-density body with very little effort. The typical pelagic shark weighs in water only a fraction of what it weighs in air. However, sharks that live primarily on the sea bottom, such as angel sharks, and have less need of lift in the water, are considerably more dense.

The nurse shark (genus *Ginglymostoma*) is recognizable by its distinct nasal barbels. Resembling fangs, the barbels are actually soft and fleshy, and give this shark a sense of touch. *Right:* Using its pharyngeal cavity, the nurse shark can produce a suction that can draw prey out of rock crevices.

The sand tiger shark (Family Odontaspididae) is easily recognized by its distinctive exposed teeth. *Opposite:* The slow-moving approach of a hornshark (genus *Heterodontus*). The hornshark often spends its entire life in one tiny area of the sea.

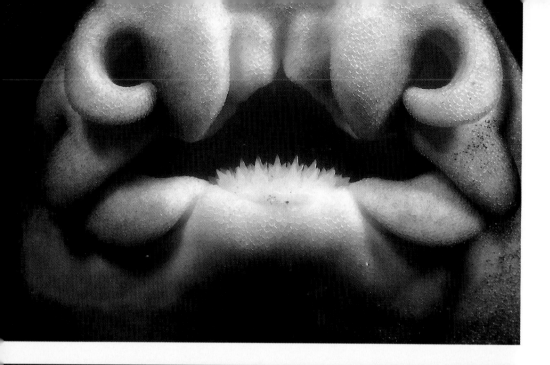

The skin of the shark is also different from most fish. Instead of scales, sharks have denticles – small, hard, stud-like protuberances containing nerve and blood vessels. These denticles, as the name implies, are made from the same material as the shark's teeth. They are curved and rough at the rear edge. Rub the shark's skin from front to back and the feeling is smooth, rub it from back to front and there is a painful feeling of sharp bristles. It is easy to be injured by a shark in this way, even if one is not subject to direct attack.

It is not known for sure if these prickly spines are for protection or if they have some hydrodynamic purpose, helping the shark move more smoothly through the water. There are also variant skin textures among different species. The bullhead shark lacks the sharp spines, while on the prickly dogfish, the spines are sharper than average – petting one would be like stroking your hand across barbed wire.

The muscles in the shark's body are attached to the skin instead of the skeleton, which allows for more variable and precise locomotion among "typical"

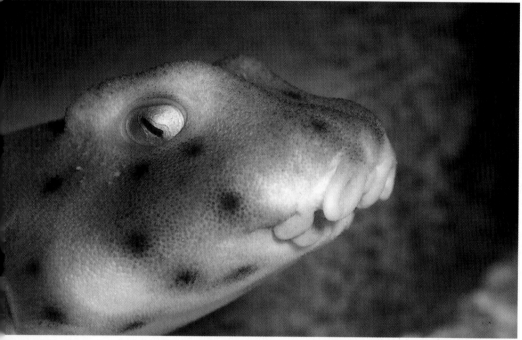

Top to bottom: **Although the hornshark (genus** *Heterodontus***) takes its name from the shape of the spines on its dorsal fins, it is also known as the "pig shark" for its oddly piglike snout. The adult horn shark grows to a size of only three feet in length. Its food of preference is the sea urchin.** *Opposite:* **The wobbegong shark (Family Orectolobidae) has the most unusual markings of any shark; it is a swirl of strangely shaped blotches, intended to help it blend in and disappear against the rocks and sand on the sea floor.**

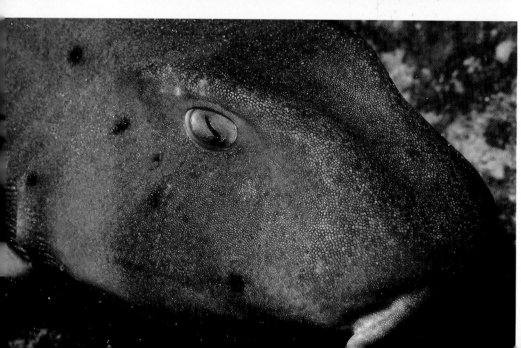

The yawning mouth of this spotted wobbegong *(Orectolobus maculatus)* is a gesture that befits this sluggish, bottom-dwelling shark. *Below:* Here is seen the unusual, paisley-like pattern of the wobbegongs.

sharks – by which we mean any of the streamlined, predatory sharks. The structure of the muscles enables the shark to maintain a casual, cruising speed, rippling along by using its whole form to propel itself. But if sudden speed and strength are needed, the shark can stiffen skin against muscle, the tail alone waving, shooting it forward at great speed – a virtual torpedo. The requiem shark is built to move with speed and efficiency when needed, its fins giving it a highly tuned ability to accelerate, turn, twist, roll, and brake.

Sharks have even greater diversity in their head shapes, none more so than the hammerhead shark. Its head is shaped laterally, with its eyes placed far apart on the ends of the left and right stalks. An even more extreme variation of the hammerhead is the winghead shark, with its wide, hammerlike head fully half the size of its entire body. A lesser-known oddity is the sawshark. Its head ends in a long, tapered snout, covered with upraised denticles – like the teeth of a saw. Not surprisingly, the "saw" is used as a weapon against

Top to bottom: **The lemon shark (***Negaprion brevirostris)* **can present great difficulties for a diver. While it is generally unaggressive in natural waters, it can turn very violent, especially within an aquarium. Scientists examine an average-sized lemon shark: Lemon sharks grow to a size of 10 feet or more, but may take as long as 15 years to reach maturity.** *Overleaf:* **The lemon shark is usually found in shallow and brackish waters. Here one is seen in the sand flats off the Bahamian island of Bimini. Overfishing will easily endanger the lemon shark's existence.**

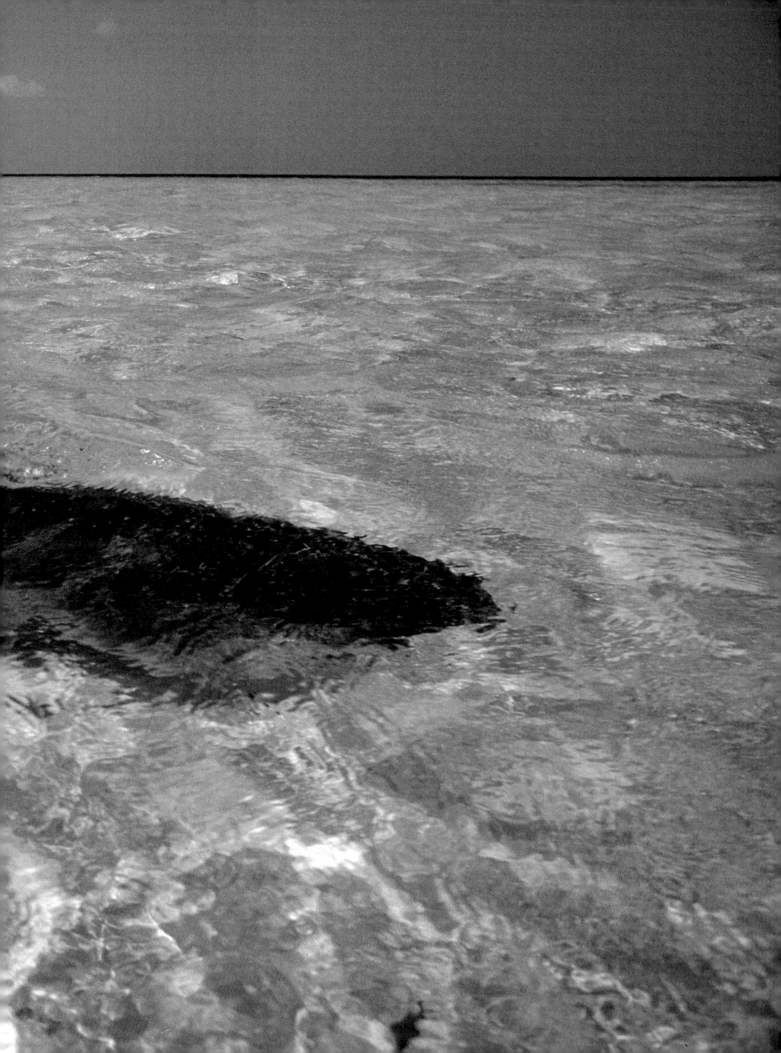

prey. The hornshark has peculiarly piggish nostrils, while the flat head of the angel shark is more reminiscent of a ray, and the obscure goblin shark is virtually a gargoyle, with protruding jaw and dagger snout.

The placement of the shark's mouth on the underside of the head is curious, as it is logical for the bottom-feeding species but not for the swimming predators, which attack their prey straight on. Scientists believe that there was a period, starting perhaps 300 million years ago, when all sharks were bottom-feeders, living on mollusks and crustaceans. With an increase in the swimming fish population, some species of shark evolved to become predators, although the mouths remained below the heads on these sharks.

Early, badly researched reports on sharks had it that they were unable to bite at anything in front of them, and even that they were forced to turn upside-down to feed. In fact, the design of the shark's mouth is much more sophisticated and, in some circumstances, frightening. The shark cannot see what it is about to bite directly in front of it, true, but its nostrils and electroreceptors on the snout deliver necessary sensory information. Sharks can indeed bite at what is in front of them: the protruding

Not to be confused with its docile cousin, the whitetip reef shark *(Triaenodon obesus)*, the oceanic whitetip *(Carcharhinus longimanus)* is extremely dangerous — some experts have called it the *most* dangerous of all. It is a fearless killer.

The mako (genus *Isurus*), reaching lengths of up to 13 feet, is one of the most highly prized catches by deep-sea fishermen. It is also one of the fastest of all underwater creatures.

snout actually rises back while the jaws are thrown forward, teeth fully exposed.

Those jaws, those teeth embody much of the mythology of terror that man has directed at the shark. And to be sure, the shark's jaws and teeth are super-efficient machinery that have made the bigger species apex predators, the top of the food chain.

The design of the jaw in the modern shark is nothing short of amazing. Its mobility comes from its not being bound to the brain-case, allowing the jaws to protrude during an attack and feeding. In an attack, the shark's head rises so that the jaws extend outward. With large prey, the shark's lower jaw hits first, holding the prey in place as the upper jaw comes forward and down, teeth digging in as the shark's head shakes violently, effectively sawing a chunk out of the prey and then tearing it away. The force of a shark's bite is tremendous – estimated at 20 tons per square inch for an eight-footer. To withstand the force of impact, the shark itself comes equipped with "shock absorbers," expanded dorsal and ventral processes that protect the spine.

The great strength of the jaws would be meaningless if they did not contain equally deadly teeth. Here again are found detailed and subtle designs, with teeth made to match the characteristic prey of a given shark. The great white shark has wide, serrated teeth made for biting out large chunks of its prey. Other sharks (such as

The gigantic whale shark *(Rhincodon typus)* has been known only since 1828, and was photographed for the first time just a few decades ago. *Below:* The whale shark is the largest fish in the sea. Lengths of 45 feet may be common, and marine biologists believe they may come larger than that!

Preceding pages: **The whale shark *(Rhincodon typus)* is a filter feeder, dining for the most part on the tiniest of marine organisms. It is a gentle giant on whom divers have hitched rides.** *This page:* **The basking shark *(Cetorhinus maximus)* is a member of the mackerel shark family, but it has much in common with the whale shark, being a filter feeder. Its great size (up to 40 feet) and enormous mouth mask a gentle nature.**

the mako, which swallows small fish whole for its diet) have thin, sharply pointed teeth used for impaling the fish. The bottom-dwelling swellshark, on the other hand, feeds on hard-shelled crustaceans, for which purpose it has small, sharp teeth.

The shape of the teeth will also vary according to the age of a particular species. Young great whites, not so likely to take on a more mature white's large prey, have the narrower, pointier teeth designed for impaling small fish.

Sharks, unlike humans, have no fear of losing a tooth. Large predators in particular blunt or break many teeth in the course of feeding, but each damaged tooth is quickly replaced by a new one. Sharks come equipped with an almost endless supply of new teeth, which grow in rows along a membrane known as a tooth bed. These "reserve teeth" simply move out into place as they are needed, thousands in a shark's lifetime.

Another long-held theory about sharks was that they had poor eyesight. Once again, much of the early research has been proven ignorant. The eyes of sharks have much variation and some remarkable capacities.

Opposite: **The blue shark *(Prionace glauca)* is a thing of deadly beauty. Preferring deep water, the blue rarely has contact with man – except for unfortunate encounters with survivors of shipwrecks and air crashes.**

Generally, active swimming predators have larger eyes, while the less active, native to shallow water, like those of the hornshark, have smaller eyes. On most sharks, the eyelids do not move, but some have a membrane that will cover and protect the eye during feeding. The reason the shark does not need an eyelid is because the pupil itself is able to control the amount of light coming in. Behind the retina of the shark's eye is a tapetum (or mirror-like plates) that reflects light into the eye's receptor cells, increasing sensitivity.

But the eyes are just one component in the shark's elaborate sensory system. The hearing of most sharks is very well developed. Although ear openings are small, sharks can hear very slight sounds and water movements, and can pick up low-frequency noises unheard by man. Scientists have shown how they can quickly summon sharks by creating pulse tones similar to that of an injured fish. The shark's sense of smell is also well developed. Experiments have shown that sharks can smell prey from great distances, even when no other sensory stimulus is involved. The olfactory sacs in the nostrils are very sensitive, constantly "testing" the water for odors. These nasal sacs have an entrance and exit for the tested water, allowing a constant, fresh flow. It takes just a thousandth of a second for the shark's sense of smell to react to stimuli, and the amount of that stimuli in the water may be infinitesimal.

Preceding pages: The blue shark *(Prionace glauca)* prefers a cool water temperature. It will swim near the surface in temperate waters, but in warmer, tropical seas, it lives at much greater depths. It is a slow, graceful swimmer, but it is also capable of sudden bursts of speed. *This page:* Blue sharks (top) practice sexual segregation. Each summer along the West Coast of America, blue males remain in the south while the females migrate to northern waters. A blue shark (bottom), known as a voracious eater, quickly dispatches a mackerel.

The shark's most intriguing sensory power – and the one most alien to man – involves electricity. Through small organs on its head, called the ampullae of Lorenzini, the shark is able to detect electrical signals. This electroreceptor system may be used in connection with the earth's magnetic field, aiding the shark in navigation, but its primary use is probably as a kind of short-range radar for finding prey, i.e., detecting the presence of camouflaged or hidden fish. Also, in the movement of attack, with its snout raised

In these photographs, a diver enters a shark cage with bait. From within the steel cage, a diver can make close observation of the more dangerous sharks in relative safety – or so it is hoped.

Preceding page: **The bloody bait begins to draw sharks to the cage. The sharks may warily circle the cage for some time before deciding to strike.** *This page:* **A blue shark (Prionace glauca) moves in an ever-tightening circle around the diver in the shark cage (top). This diver (bottom) demonstrates the effectiveness of the Neptunic shark suit against the attack of a blue shark.**

and its eyes rolling back or covered for protection, the shark's electric detectors will "tune in" on the prey's electro-field. Scientists have found that when sharks have seemingly attacked inanimate objects like boats and shark cages in baited water, it is not out of some savage urge to eat *anything* but due instead to the strange and con-fusing electric signals surrounding the bait. Under ordinary condi-tions, the shark makes extraor-dinarily effective use of its whole elaborate and interconnecting sensory system.

Very few sharks are ordinarily dangerous to man. Out of the hundreds of species, perhaps 10 or a dozen have been

Preceding page: A good shark suit increases the safety margin of any diver, and allows marine biologists a closer study of their subject. But the powerful force of a large, attacking shark can still do great damage to any free-swimming diver. *This page:* A wide-angle lens conveys the tension-filled point-of-view of a photographer inside a tiny shark cage. The steel bars of the cage seem a paltry defense against a head-on attack by an angry blacktip shark *(Carcharhinus limbatus)*.

For many, the dorsal fin of a great white shark *(Carcharodon carcharias)* slicing through the ocean's surface is an emblem of terror.

known to attack without provocation. These include the great white and assorted members of the requiem shark family, such as tiger shark, blue shark, bull, and grey reef. Without a doubt, these sharks have perpetrated some horrible attacks on humans. Bathers, divers, shipwreck victims have been bitten and gouged severely, had limbs torn from their bodies, and have been swallowed nearly whole. But the number of these incidents is tiny in proportion to the worldwide "shark attack" hysteria that has so often erupted. In Australia, for instance, where the long coastline hosts numerous large predators including the great white, the beaches are considered among the world's most dangerous because of shark attacks. Yet 90 years of record-keeping show only a few hundred shark attacks and 100 fatalities. Of course, one such incident is one too many, but it was discovered that nearly as many serious dog attacks had occurred in the same period, and the number of fatalities in car accidents was, of course, much higher.

Top to bottom: **The great white shark is a menacing apex predator; it will eagerly attack and devour creatures its own size, including sea lions, seals, other sharks, and, occasionally, humans. While this great white shark bares its dagger-like teeth to a piece of bait, one can see the mictating membrane that protects the shark's eyes during an attack. A moment of extreme danger is caught on film: A photographer-diver has ventured out of the shark cage just as a great white makes a sudden, unexpected appearance.** *Overleaf:* **The great white shark has been the cause of more hysteria and fear than almost any other creature on earth — except, perhaps, for the human creature.**

The most dangerous – certainly the most famous – of man-eaters is the great white shark. Great whites have taken sizable chunks out of boats and surf boards as well as out of humans. Scientists believe most of these attacks are due to confusion on the shark's part – it may think the objects are large sea mammals (one of its favorite foods). The great white seldom actually eats its human victims. It will often take a vicious bite and then circle around as the victim dies.

But even among confirmed man-eaters, the most attacks occur when the human has invaded and disturbed the shark's natural habitat – and our species has not had a reputation for respecting the territorial rights of any species, including our own.

In point of fact, the shark is in more danger from us than we are from it. About 12 men and women are killed by sharks each year worldwide. In the same year, man kills – for food, sport or "thrills"– approximately 100 million sharks. This slaughter has already begun to bring some species of shark close to extinction. But a fish with such a notorious reputation as the shark's often has trouble receiving the kind of national and international protection offered to other endangered or over-hunted animals. Perhaps, though, as more people begin to understand the unique and beautiful attributes of the shark, and put its predatory nature into a realistic perspective, something will be done, before it is too late.

Preceding pages: The teeth of the great white shark *(Carcharodon carcharias)* are triangular, with razor-sharp serrations. As its jaws close, the upper and lower teeth come together like scissors. The great white does not chew its food – it merely bites and swallows. *This page:* Off the coast of northern Australia, a great white shark (top) raises its huge and powerful head above the sea. Although it has been found in the tropics, the great white prefers the cooler waters of temperate zones. Here, a great white shark swims amid a school of tommy-roughs (bottom). It seems an unnaturally gentle image for the notorious "white death," but in fact, the great white's reputation as a bloodthirsty man-killer is greatly exaggerated. Only a handful of humans are attacked each year and of these, most survive.

As it is the most famous of the hundreds of types of shark, the great white is routinely blamed for attacks and killings done by other shark species.

A great white shark *(Carcharodon carcharias)* approaches a shark cage. The great white is not merely a powerful creature, but one of great intelligence, possessing advanced sensory equipment.

While some species of shark are quite social, the great white spends most of its life in solitude, a lone predator. *Overleaf:* A great white feeds on bait suspended from a shark cage. The cages are designed to withstand enormous pressure, but large great whites — which can weigh over 3,000 pounds — have, on occasion, torn such cages to pieces.

Preceding page: The great white shark *(Carcharodon carcharias)* is one of the earth's longest-lived creatures, with an ancestry of 60 million years. *This page:* Here is seen the blood-spattered, gaping mouth of a great white, with its spikelike teeth of nightmarish size and sharpness.

A shark's jaws have great mobility. Not bound to the braincase, the jaws can extend outward from the face when the shark attacks its food. *Opposite:* Here, rising six feet straight out of the water to rip into a dangling bait, a great white shark *(Charcharodon carcharias)* shows both grace and fury.

Index of Photography